HA! HA! HA!

Over 350 very funny jokes

Illustrated by Tim Archbold,
Mik Brown *and* Tania Hurt-Newton

KINGFISHER

WHO'S THERE?

OVER 100 CLASSIC KNOCK KNOCK JOKES

• Illustrated by Tim Archbold •

KNOCK KNOCK!
Who's there?
Police.
Police who?
Police open up the door.

KNOCK KNOCK!
Who's there?
Isabelle.
Isabelle who?
Isabelle necessary on a bicycle?

KNOCK KNOCK!
Who's there?
Luke.
Luke who?
Luke through the keyhole and you'll see.

KNOCK KNOCK!
Who's there?
Ya.
Ya who?
I didn't know you were a cowboy!

KNOCK KNOCK!
Who's there?
Mr.
Mr who?
Missed her at the bus stop.

KNOCK KNOCK!
Who's there?
Boo!
Boo who?
Don't cry, it's only a joke.

KNOCK KNOCK!
Who's there?
Atch.
Atch who?
Sorry, I didn't know you had a cold.

KNOCK KNOCK!
Who's there?
Micky.
Micky who?
Micky is lost so that's why I'm knocking.

KNOCK KNOCK!
Who's there?
Teresa.
Teresa who?
Teresa green.

KNOCK KNOCK!
Who's there?
Noah.
Noah who?
Noah don't know who you are either.

KNOCK KNOCK!
Who's there?
Justin.
Justin who?
Justin time for the party!

KNOCK KNOCK!
Who's there?
Banana.
Banana who?
KNOCK KNOCK!
Who's there?
Banana.
Banana who?
KNOCK KNOCK!
Who's there?
Orange.
Orange who?
Orange you glad I didn't say banana?

KNOCK KNOCK!
Who's there?
Ken.
Ken who?
Ken I come in or do I have to climb through the window?

KNOCK KNOCK!
Who's there?
Bernadette.
Bernadette who?
Bernadette all my dinner and I'm starving!

Will you remember me tomorrow?
Yes
Will you remember me in a week?
Yes
Will you remember me in a month?
Yes
Will you remember me in a year?
Yes
KNOCK KNOCK!
Who's there?
Forgotten me already?

KNOCK KNOCK!
Who's there?
Major.
Major who?
Major answer didn't I?

KNOCK KNOCK!
Who's there?
Howard.
Howard who?
Howard you like to be outside for a change?

KNOCK KNOCK!
Who's there?
Senior.
Senior who?
Senior so nosy, I'm not going to tell you.

KNOCK KNOCK!
Who's there?
Wilma.
Wilma who?
Wilma lunch be ready soon?

KNOCK KNOCK!
Who's there?
Isaac.
Isaac who?
Isaac coming in!

KNOCK KNOCK!
Who's there?
Alfred.
Alfred who?
Alfred the needle if you sew.

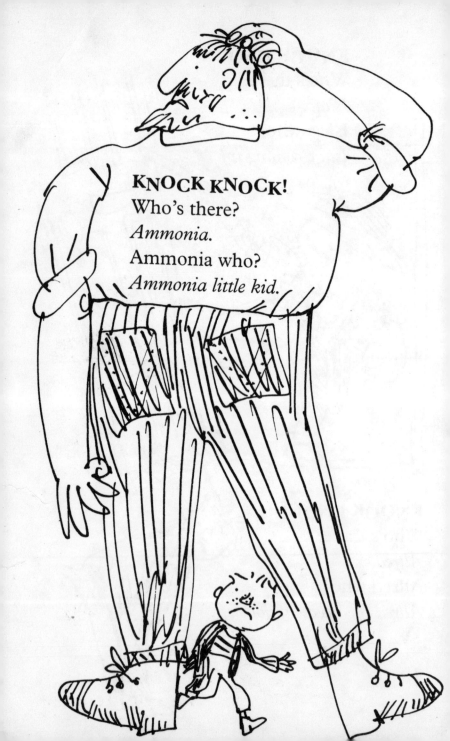

KNOCK KNOCK!
Who's there?
Ammonia.
Ammonia who?
Ammonia little kid.

KNOCK KNOCK!
Who's there?
Amos.
Amos who?
Amos-quito bit me.

KNOCK KNOCK!
Who's there?
Andy.
Andy who?
Andy bit me again.

KNOCK KNOCK!
Who's there?
Anna.
Anna who?
Anna-ther mosquito!

KNOCK KNOCK!
Who's there?
Tennis.
Tennis who?
Tennis five plus five.

KNOCK KNOCK!
Who's there?
Cash.
Cash who?
I knew you were nuts.

KNOCK KNOCK!
Who's there?
Felix.
Felix who?
Felix my ice cream, I'll lick his.

KNOCK KNOCK!
Who's there?
Fletcher.
Fletcher who?
Fletcher self go!

KNOCK KNOCK!
Who's there?
Arthur.
Arthur who?
Arthur any more biscuits in the tin?

KNOCK KNOCK!
Who's there?
Cynthia.
Cynthia who?
Cynthia been away, I've missed you.

KNOCK KNOCK!
Who's there?
Viola.
Viola who?
Viola sudden don't you know me?

KNOCK KNOCK!
Who's there?
Irma.
Irma who?
Irma big girl now.

KNOCK KNOCK!
Who's there?
William.
William who?
Williamind your own business.

KNOCK KNOCK!
Who's there?
Weirdo.
Weirdo who?
Weirdo you think you're going?

KNOCK KNOCK!
Who's there?
Handsome.
Handsome who?
Handsome spaghetti through the keyhole and
I'll tell you.

KNOCK KNOCK!
Who's there?
Nana.
Nana who?
Nana your business.

KNOCK KNOCK!
Who's there?
Yvonne.
Yvonne who?
Yvonne to be alone!

KNOCK KNOCK!
Who's there?
Alison.
Alison who?
Alison to my radio.

KNOCK KNOCK!
Who's there?
Scot.
Scot who?
Scot nothing to do with you.

KNOCK KNOCK!
Who's there?
Irish stew.
Irish stew who?
Irish stew in the name of the law!

KNOCK KNOCK!
Who's there?
Lena.
Lena who?
Lena little closer and I'll tell you.

KNOCK KNOCK!
Who's there?
Cows.
Cows who?
Cows go moo not who.

KNOCK KNOCK!
Who's there?
Europe.
Europe who?
Europe to no good.

KNOCK KNOCK!
Who's there?
Myth.
Myth who?
Myth you too.

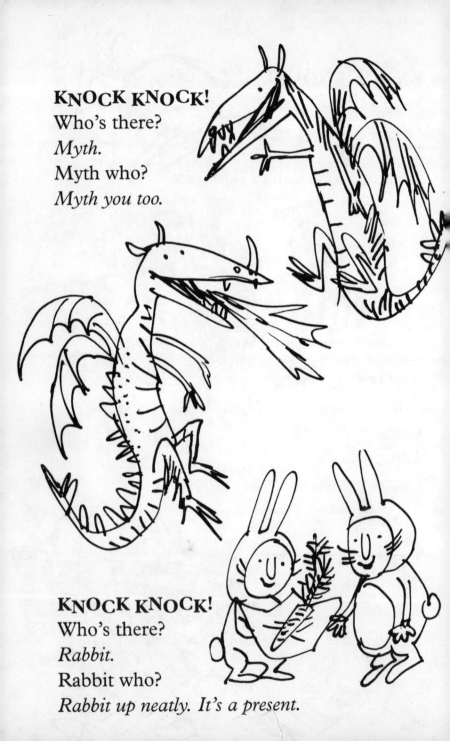

KNOCK KNOCK!
Who's there?
Rabbit.
Rabbit who?
Rabbit up neatly. It's a present.

KNOCK KNOCK!
Who's there?
A little old lady.
A little old lady who?
I didn't know you could yodel.

KNOCK KNOCK!
Who's there?
Lionel.
Lionel who?
Lionel get you nowhere.

KNOCK KNOCK!
Who's there?
Jester.
Jester who?
Jester minute,
I'm trying to
find my key.

KNOCK KNOCK!
Who's there?
Snow.
Snow who?
Snow use, I've forgotten my key again.

KNOCK KNOCK!
Who's there?
Adelia.
Adelia who?
Adelia the cards and we'll play poker.

KNOCK KNOCK!
Who's there?
Eva.
Eva who?
*Eva you're deaf or your doorbell isn't
working.*

KNOCK KNOCK!
Who's there?
Phyllis.
Phyllis who?
*Phyllis in on
the news.*

KNOCK KNOCK!
Who's there?
Oscar.
Oscar who?
Oscar silly question, get a silly answer.

KNOCK KNOCK!
Who's there?
Francis.
Francis who?
Francis on the other side of the Channel.

KNOCK KNOCK!
Who's there?
Dimitri.
Dimitri who?
Dimitri is where lamb chops grow.

KNOCK KNOCK!
Who's there?
Scold.
Scold who?
Scold outside.

KNOCK KNOCK!
Who's there?
Jamaica.
Jamaica who?
Jamaica mistake?

KNOCK KNOCK!
Who's there?
Leaf.
Leaf who?
Leaf me alone!

KNOCK KNOCK!
Who's there?
Turnip.
Turnip who?
Turnip the heat,
it's cold in here.

KNOCK KNOCK!
Who's there?
Warrior.
Warrior who?
Warrior been all my life?

KNOCK KNOCK!
Who's there?
Midas.
Midas who?
Midas well open the door.

KNOCK KNOCK!
Who's there?
Theodore.
Theodore who?
Theodore is shut, please open it!

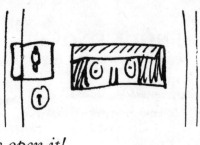

KNOCK KNOCK!
Who's there?
Olivia.
Olivia who?
Olivia but I've lost my key.

KNOCK KNOCK!
Who's there?
Gladys.
Gladys who?
Gladys Saturday, aren't you?

KNOCK KNOCK!
Who's there?
Wheelbarrow.
Wheelbarrow who?
*Wheelbarrow some
money and go to Mexico!*

KNOCK KNOCK!
Who's there?
Miniature.
Miniature who?
Miniature open the door, I'll tell you.

KNOCK KNOCK!
Who's there?
Congo.
Congo who?
Congo on meeting like this.

KNOCK KNOCK!
Who's there?
Jaws.
Jaws who?
Jaws truly.

KNOCK KNOCK!
Who's there?
Pasture.
Pasture who?
Pasture bedtime, isn't it?

KNOCK KNOCK!
Who's there?
Sherwood.
Sherwood who?
Sherwood like to come in, please.

KNOCK KNOCK!
Who's there?
Aardvark.
Aardvark who?
Aardvark a hundred miles
for just one of your smiles.

KNOCK KNOCK!
Who's there?
Gorilla.
Gorilla who?
*Gorilla me some
cheese on toast,
please.*

KNOCK KNOCK!
Who's there?
Stopwatch.
Stopwatch who?
Stopwatch you're doing right now!

KNOCK KNOCK!
Who's there?
Doughnut.
Doughnut who?
Doughnut open until Christmas.

KNOCK KNOCK!
Who's there?
Emma.
Emma who?
Emma bit cold out here, can you let me in?

KNOCK KNOCK!
Who's there?
Tyrone.
Tyrone who?
Tyrone shoelaces.

KNOCK KNOCK!
Who's there?
Stan.
Stan who?
Stan back or I'll shoot.

KNOCK KNOCK!
Who's there?
Nuisance.
Nuisance who?
What's nuisance yesterday?

KNOCK KNOCK!
Who's there?
Tuna.
Tuna who?
Tuna piano and it'll sound better.

KNOCK KNOCK!
Who's there?
Alli.
Alli who?
Alligator, that's who.

KNOCK KNOCK!
Who's there?
Dawn.
Dawn who?
Dawn leave me out here in the cold.

KNOCK KNOCK!
Who's there?
You.
You who?
Did you call?

KNOCK KNOCK!
Who's there?
Pyjamas.
Pyjamas who?
Pyjamas around me and hold me tight.

KNOCK KNOCK!
Who's there?
Sarah.
Sarah who?
Sarah doctor in the house?

KNOCK KNOCK!
Who's there?
Dishes.
Dishes who?
Dishes a very bad joke.

KNOCK KNOCK!
Who's there?
Oslo.
Oslo who?
Oslo down, what's the hurry?

KNOCK KNOCK!
Who's there?
Watson.
Watson who?
Watson television?

KNOCK KNOCK!
Who's there?
Says.
Says who?
Says me, that's who!

KNOCK KNOCK!
Who's there?
Aladdin.
Aladdin who?
Aladdin the street wants a word with you.

KNOCK KNOCK!
Who's there?
Amy.
Amy who?
Amy fraid I've forgotten.

KNOCK KNOCK!
Who's there?
Eddie.
Eddie who?
Eddie body home?

KNOCK KNOCK!
Who's there?
Beezer.
Beezer who?
Beezer black and yellow.

KNOCK KNOCK!
Who's there?
Shirley.
Shirley who?
Shirley you must know me by now.

KNOCK KNOCK!
Who's there?
Adair.
Adair who?
Adair once but now I'm bald.

KNOCK KNOCK!
Who's there?
Witches.
Witches who?
Witches the way to go home?

KNOCK KNOCK!
Who's there?
Dummy.
Dummy who?
Dummy a favour and get lost.

This is your illustrator speaking: it's 3 a.m. and here I am drawing knock knock jokes. I use an old-fashioned dip pen and ink, which scratches and splatters on the paper.

This is Sam, my spaniel. He has just eaten six chocolate biscuits, a box of coloured crayons and two paintbrushes. That's why he's got a peculiar look on his face.

Also, I think he's heard one too many jokes....

Tim.

Mik Brown's
HORRIBLY
SILLY
JOKES

Why were the elephants thrown out of the swimming-pool?

Because they couldn't hold their trunks up.

How do you know when there's an elephant in the refrigerator?

When you can't shut the door.

THUD!

What do you get if you cross an elephant with a kangaroo?

Great big holes all over Australia.

What do you call an elephant that flies?

A jumbo jet.

Why did the elephant paint himself different colours?

Because he wanted to hide in the crayon box.

How does an elephant get down from a tree?

He sits on a leaf and waits for autumn.

**What did the elephant
say to the orange?**

Let's play squash.

**Why are elephants
so wrinkled?**

Have you ever tried ironing one?

One snake said to another:

"Are we supposed to be poisonous?"
"Why?"
"Because I've just bitten my lip."

What do you get if you cross a snake with a magician?

Abra da cobra.

What's green and slimy and goes *hith*?

A snake with a lisp.

**What do polar bears
have for lunch?**

Ice burgers.

**What gets wet
as it dries?**

A towel.

**What animal do you look
like in the bath?**

A little
bear.

What's white outside, green inside and hops?

A frog sandwich.

Where do tadpoles turn into frogs?

In the croakroom.

FREDA: "Will I be able to read with these glasses?"

FRED: "You certainly will."

FREDA: "That's good. I couldn't before."

Where do you take a frog with bad eyesight?

To the hoptician.

What's red and flies and wobbles at the same time?

A jellycopter.

What's green and can jump a mile a minute?

A frog with hiccups.

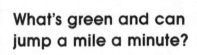

Why are goldfish red?

The water makes
them rusty.

What did the sardine call the submarine?

A can of people.

TEACHER: "You should have been here
at 9 o'clock."

PUPIL: "Why, what happened?"

What kind of noise annoys an oyster?

A noisy noise annoys an oyster.

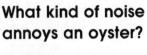

What's yellow and highly dangerous?

Shark-infested custard.

What do you get from a bad-tempered shark?

As far away as possible.

If athletes get athlete's foot, what do astronauts get?

Missile-toe.

What do astronauts eat for lunch?

Launch-meat sandwiches.

What do you call a mad astronaut?

An astronut.

How do you get a baby astronaut to sleep?

You rock-et.

SPLOP!

What did the astronaut see in his frying pan?

An unidentified frying object.

What do you give a sick pig?

Oinkment.

What kind of tie does a pig wear?

A pig-sty.

Why is getting up in the morning like a pig's tail?

Because it's twirly (too early).

How do you stop a skunk from smelling?

Hold its nose.

**What do you get
if you cross a
bear with a skunk?**

Winnie the Pooh.

**What do skunks have that no
other animals have?**

Baby skunks.

"Waiter, this soup tastes funny."

"Then why aren't you laughing?"

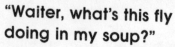

"Waiter, what's this fly doing in my soup?"

"Looks like it's learning to swim, sir."

"Waiter, there's a small slug on this lettuce."

"Sorry, sir, shall I get you a bigger one?"

"Waiter, there's a mouse in my hamburger."

"Don't shout, sir, or everyone will want one."

"Waiter, do you have frogs' legs?"

"No, sir, I've always walked like this."

"Waiter, there's a caterpillar on my salad."

"Don't worry, sir, there's no extra charge."

"Waiter, there's a fly in my soup."

"Don't worry, sir, that spider on your bread will soon get rid of it."

"Waiter, your thumb is in my soup."

"That's okay, madam, it's not hot."

"Waiter, this coffee is terrible — it tastes like earth!"

"Yes, sir, it was ground yesterday."

"Waiter, is there soup on the menu?"

"No, madam, I wiped it off."

"Waiter, this egg is bad."

"Don't blame me, madam, I only laid the table."

"Waiter, bring me something to eat, and make it snappy."

"How about a crocodile sandwich, sir."

What did the pony say when he coughed?

"Excuse me, I'm just a little horse."

What did the hungry donkey say when it had only thistles to eat?

"Thist-le have to do."

Who always goes to bed with shoes on?

A horse.

How do you start a flea race?

1, 2, flea, go.

What did the earwig say when it fell off the cliff?

"'Ere we go."

What lies down a hundred feet in the air?

A centipede.

What bee can never be understood?

A mumble-bee.

Why do bees hum?

Because they don't know the words.

What is the biggest ant?

An elephant.

How can you tell which end of a worm is which?

Tickle its middle and see which end smiles.

When did the fly fly?

When the spider spied her.

When the dentist put his fingers in the crocodile's mouth to see how many teeth it had, what did the crocodile do?

It closed its mouth to see how many fingers the dentist had.

What's a crocodile's favourite card game?

Snap.

What do you call a sick crocodile?

An illigator.

**What's the difference
between a crocodile
and a postbox?**

If you don't know, watch out
when you next post a letter.

**Have you heard
the joke about
the watermelon?**

It's pitiful.

**What's green and
dangerous and
good at arithmetic?**

A crocodile
with a
calculator.

How do you tell a rabbit from a gorilla?

A rabbit doesn't look like a gorilla.

What is a twip?

A twip is what a wabbit makes when he wides a twain.

What do you get if you pour hot water down a rabbit hole?

Hot-cross bunnies.

"If I give you three rabbits . . .

. . . and then I give you two rabbits . . .

. . . how many rabbits will you have?"

"Six."   "Six?"

"Yes, I've got one already."

What do you call a gorilla wearing headphones?

Anything, he can't hear you.

Why does a monkey scratch himself?

Because he's the only one who knows where it itches.

How do you catch a monkey?

Hang upside down in a tree and make a noise like a banana.

Why are monsters forgetful?

Because everything you tell them goes in one ear and out the others.

Why did the monster knit herself three socks?

Because she grew another foot.

What's the difference between a huge, ugly, smelly monster and a sweet?

People like sweets.

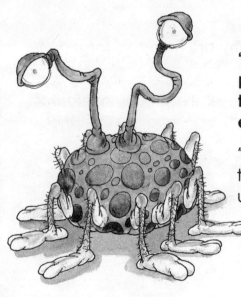

"What has a purple-spotted body, ten hairy legs and big eyes on stalks?"

"I don't know, but there's one crawling up your leg."

What do you say when you meet a two-headed monster?

"Hello, hello!"

What is the best way to speak to a monster?

From a long distance.

What's big, red and prickly, has three eyes and eats rocks?

A big, red, prickly, three-eyed rock-eater.

How does a monster count to fifteen?

On its fingers.

TIC!
TOC!

What goes tick-tock, bow-wow, tick-tock, bow-wow?

A watch-dog.

What did the puppy say when it sat on sandpaper?

"Ruff!"

GIRL: "I've lost my dog."

BOY: "Why don't you put an ad in the paper?"

GIRL: "Don't be silly! My dog can't read."

Why does a dog wag its tail?

Because no one will wag it for him.

"Doctor, doctor, I feel like a bell."

"Take these and, if they don't work, give me a ring."

"Doctor, doctor, I keep thinking I'm a dustbin."

"Don't talk rubbish."

"Doctor, doctor, I keep forgetting things."

"When did this start happening?"

"When did what start happening?"

"Doctor, doctor, my hair keeps falling out. Can you give me something to keep it in?"

"How about a paper bag?"

"Doctor, doctor, I feel like an apple."

"Come over here, I won't bite you."

Doctor, doctor, I keep thinking I'm invisible."

"Who said that?"

"Doctor, doctor, I feel like a pair of curtains."

"Pull yourself together."

"Doctor, doctor, I've got a terrible sore throat."

"Go over to the window and stick your tongue out."

"Will that help my throat?"

"No, I just don't like the man next door."

"Doctor, doctor, everybody ignores me."

"Next, please."

"If I had eight hedgehogs in one hand and seven hedgehogs in the other, what would I have?"

"Big hands."

Why did the hedgehog wear red boots?

Because his brown ones were at the mender's.

**What did the
hedgehog say
to the cactus?**

"Is that you, Mama?"

**Where would you find
a prehistoric cow?**

In a moo-seum.

**What do you get if you cross
a cow, a sheep and a goat?**

The Milky Baa Kid.

**Which cows have
the shortest legs?**

The smallest ones.

Why did the cow go over the hill?

Because it couldn't go under it.

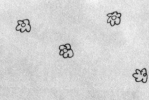

Where do cows go on a Saturday night?

To the moo-vies.

What goes OOM OOM?

A cow walking backwards.

What do you call a bull asleep on the ground?

A bulldozer.

FIRST COW: "Moo"

SECOND COW: "Baa-a-a."

FIRST COW: "What do you mean 'Baa-a-a'?"

SECOND COW: "I'm learning a foreign language."

**What's white,
has four legs
and a trunk?**

A mouse going
on holiday.

**What do angry mice send each other
at Christmas?**

Cross-mouse cards.

**What's brown,
has four legs
and a trunk?**

A mouse coming
back from holiday.

What do mice do in the daytime?

Mousework.

How can you tell one cat from another?

Look them up in a catalogue.

What's grey, has four legs and weighs one-and-a-half pounds?

A fat mouse.

What has the head of a cat, the tail of a cat, but is not a cat?

A kitten.

What works in a circus, does somersaults and meows?

An acrocat.

There are ten copycats in a car, one gets out, how many are left?

None.

Why do cats have furry coats?

Because they'd look silly in plastic macs.

Spell "mousetrap" in three letters.

C-A-T.

How do you stop your dog barking in the hall?

Put it outside.

"Your dog's been chasing a man on a bicycle."

"Don't be silly! My dog can't ride a bicycle."

GIRL: "I've found a penguin."

BOY: "Why don't you take it to the zoo?"

GIRL: "I took it to the zoo yesterday.
Today we're going to the cinema."

**Why don't ducks tell jokes
when they're flying?**

Because they would
quack up.

**Why do birds fly south
in the winter?**

Because it's too
far to walk.

What do you get if you cross a parrot with an alligator?

Something that bites your hand off and says, "Who's a pretty boy then?"

WHO'S A PRETTY BOY THEN?

What do you call a crate of ducks?

A box of quackers.

"Mummy, mummy, I've just swallowed my mouth organ!"

"Just be glad you don't play the piano."

GULP!

Why did the mother kangaroo scold her baby?

Because he'd been eating biscuits in bed.

JIM: "What's the matter?"

TOM: "My new shoes hurt."

JIM: "That's because you've got them on the wrong feet."

TOM: "Well, they're the only feet I have."

What does an angry kangaroo do?

Get hopping mad.

SON: "Can I have another glass of water?"

FATHER: "Another? This will be your tenth!"

SON: "I know, but my room's on fire."

What do you get if you cross a kangaroo with a sheep?

A woolly jumper.

Where do you find hippos?

It depends where you left them.

Which animal is always laughing?

A happy-potamus.

How do you tell the difference between a hippo and a banana?

If it's a hippo, you can't pick it up.

What does a hippo have if its head is hot, one foot is cold and it sees spots?

A polka-dotted sock over its head.

Where did Napoleon keep his armies?

Up his sleevies.

What pet makes the loudest noise?

A trumpet.

Where did Humpty Dumpty leave his hat?

Humpty dumped his hat on the wall.

What has two arms, two wings, two tails, three heads, three bodies and eight legs?

A man on a horse holding a chicken.

Mik Brown first started collecting jokes when he lived on a farm. His pigs, goats, sheep and chickens would tell him their funniest jokes as he cleaned out their sties and pens, and even agreed to pose for his drawings. An unfortunate incident involving a chicken and a cement mixer led to Mik leaving the farm, but he continues to collect jokes from his younger children, Zoe and Izaac, and their pets – four rats, a snake and a big black Newfoundland dog.

ELEPHANTASTIC!

A TRUNKFUL OF UNFORGETTABLE JOKES

illustrated by

TANIA HURT-NEWTON

Why do elephants want to be alone?
Because two's a crowd.

What's grey and moves at
a hundred miles an hour?
*A jet-propelled
elephant.*

What's big and grey
and wears a mask?
*The Elephantom of
the Opera.*

What's grey with red
spots?
*An elephant with the
measles.*

What's grey and never
needs ironing?
A drip-dry elephant.

What's big and red and grey?
A sunburnt elephant.

What is grey, stands in a river during a storm and doesn't get wet?
An elephant with an umbrella.

What's grey and goes round and round?
An elephant in a washing machine.

What's grey and powdery?
Instant elephant mix.

What's grey and
highly dangerous?
*An elephant with a
machine gun.*

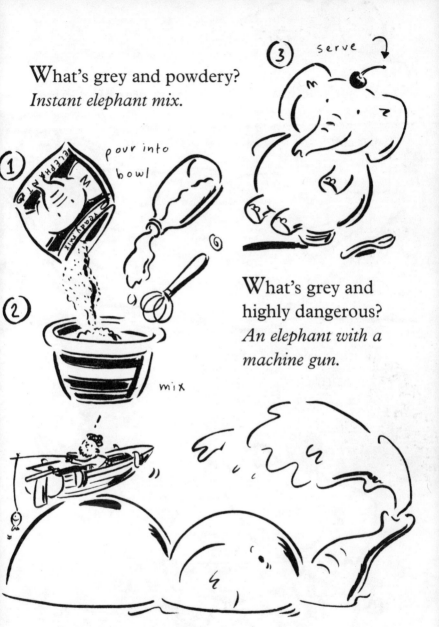

What's big and grey and lives in Scotland?
The Loch Ness Elephant.

What's yellow on the outside and grey on the inside?
An elephant disguised as a banana.

What's big and grey and protects you from the rain?
An umbrellaphant.

What's grey, wrinkly and has sixteen wheels?
An elephant on roller-skates.

What's big, grey and flies straight up?
An elecopter.

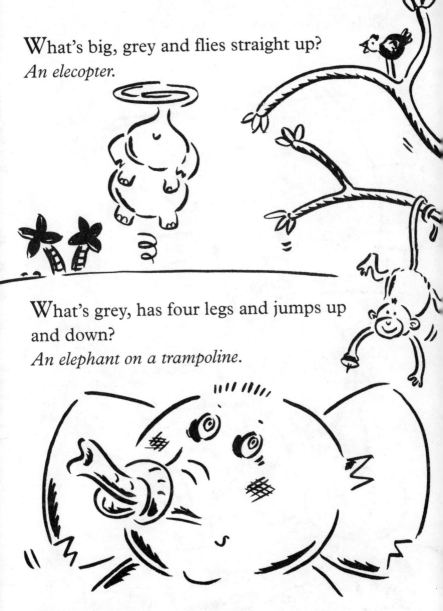

What's grey, has four legs and jumps up and down?
An elephant on a trampoline.

What's bright red and weighs four tonnes?
An elephant holding its breath.

What's blue and has big ears?
An elephant at the North Pole.

What's grey and
wrinkly and jumps
every twenty seconds?
*An elephant with
hiccups.*

What goes up slowly
but comes down fast?
An elephant in a lift.

restaurant / bar

stock room

What has three tails,
seven feet and four
trunks?
*An elephant with spare
parts.*

What's as big as an
elephant but weighs
nothing?

An elephant's shadow.

What's grey and lights up?
An electric elephant.

What's grey but turns red?
An embarrassed elephant.

What's grey, carries a bunch of flowers, and cheers you up when you're ill?
A Get-wellephant.

What's big and grey with horns?
An elephant marching band.

What's grey, has a wand, huge wings, and gives money to elephants?
The Tusk fairy.

What's grey, beautiful and wears glass slippers?
Cinderelephant.

Why is a sneezing elephant like a spy?
They both have a code in the head.

What pills do you give an elephant that
can't sleep?
Trunkquillizers.

A boy with an elephant on his head went to
see a doctor. The doctor said, "You know,
you really need help."

"*Yes I do,*" the elephant cried, "*get this kid
off my foot!*"

What's the difference between an elephant and a bad pupil?
One rarely bites, the other barely writes.

How do you tell the difference between a mouse and an elephant?
Try picking them up!

What's the difference between an elephant and a piece of paper?
You can't make a paper aeroplane out of an elephant.

What's the difference between a sick elephant and seven days?

One is a weak one, the other is one week.

What's the difference between an elephant and a banana?

Have you ever tried to peel an elephant?

What's the difference between an elephant and a gooseberry?

A gooseberry is green.

Why are elephants grey?
So you can tell them from flamingoes.

What's the difference between an elephant and a flea?
An elephant can have fleas but a flea can't have elephants.

Jambo

namaste

What's the difference between an African and an Indian elephant?
About three thousand miles.

What's worse than an elephant with a sore trunk?
A centipede with sore feet.

Why is an elephant large, grey and wrinkled?
Because if it was small, white and round it would be an aspirin.

ELEPHANT KEEPER: "My elephant's not
  well. Do you know a good animal doctor?"
ZOO KEEPER: "No, I'm afraid all the doctors
  I know are people."

PATIENT: Doctor, doctor, I keep seeing pink
  and yellow elephants.
DOCTOR: Have you seen a psychiatrist?
PATIENT: No, only pink and yellow elephants.

What kind of elephants live in Antarctica?
Cold ones.

Why do elephants have trunks?
Because they'd look silly carrying suitcases.

How do you get five elephants into a small car?
Two in the back, two in the front and one in the glove compartment.

How does an elephant get out of a small car?
The same way he got in.

Why did the elephant cross the road?
Because the chicken was having a day off.

What do you call an elephant at the
North Pole?
Lost.

Which takes less time to get ready for a trip, an elephant or a rooster?
A rooster - he only takes his comb.

What did the hotel manager say to the elephant who couldn't pay his bill?
"Pack your trunk and clear out."

How do you get an elephant into a matchbox?
Take all the matches out first.

How can you tell if an elephant has been in your fridge?
Footprints in the butter.

What did the grape say when the elephant stepped on it?
Nothing. It just let out a wine.

How do you know if there's an elephant in your dessert?
You get very lumpy ice cream!

"I know an elephant who lives on garlic alone."
"I'm not surprised he lives alone if all he eats is garlic."

Why are elephants wiser than chickens?
Ever heard of Kentucky Fried Elephant?

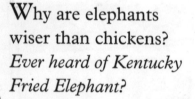

Why do elephants eat raw food?
Because they don't know how to cook.

Have you heard about
the elephant who went
on a crash diet?
*He wrecked a bus, three
cars and a fire engine.*

Why did the elephant
eat candles?
For light refreshment.

What do you do with
a green elephant?
Wait until it ripens.

Why did the elephant
sleep in a bowl of
salad dressing?
*So he'd wake up
really oily.*

What do invisible
elephants drink?
Evaporated milk.

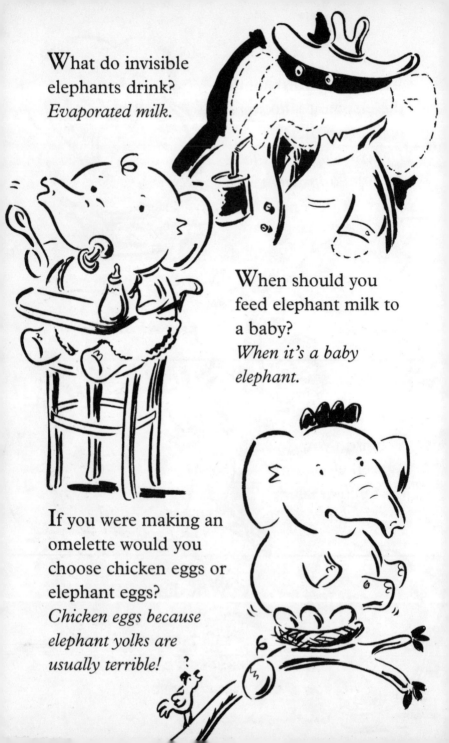

When should you
feed elephant milk to
a baby?
*When it's a baby
elephant.*

If you were making an
omelette would you
choose chicken eggs or
elephant eggs?
*Chicken eggs because
elephant yolks are
usually terrible!*

An elephant walked into a cafe and ordered a strawberry milkshake. He drank it in one gulp, paid and left.

The customers in the cafe couldn't believe their eyes. One of them said to the waitress, "What an amazing elephant! Has he done that before?"

"Oh, no," said the waitress. "Normally he has a small coke."

How do you know peanuts are fattening?
Have you ever seen a skinny elephant?

What did Tarzan say when he saw the elephants coming? *"Here come the elephants!"*

What's the best way to see a charging herd of elephants? *On television!*

Why don't elephants like playing cards in the jungle? *Because of all the cheetahs.*

"My elephant plays chess with me."

"How amazing! It must be a really intelligent animal."

"Not really. I've won three games to two so far today."

JIM: "My homework's really difficult tonight –
I've got to write an essay on the elephant."
JOHN: "Well, for a start, you're going to need
a very big ladder..."

Why do elephants do well in school?
Because they have a lot of grey matter.

TEACHER: "To which family does the
elephant belong?"
PUPIL: "I don't know, nobody I know
owns one."

(A) student

"How do you spell elephant?"

"E-l-l-e-e-f-a-n-t."

"That's not how the dictionary spells it."

"You didn't ask me how the dictionary spelt it."

TEACHER: "Name six wild animals."
PUPIL: "Two lions and four elephants."

TEACHER: "Where would you find an elephant?"
PUPIL: "You don't have to find them – they're too big to lose."

Tarzan was tired when he came home.
"What have you been doing?" asked Jane.
"Chasing a herd of elephants on vines."
"Really?" said Jane. "I thought elephants stayed on the ground."

Why shouldn't you go into the jungle at midday?
Because that's when elephants practise parachuting.

What is an easy way to get a wild elephant?
Buy a tame one and annoy it.

What do you call an
elephant that's small
and pink?
A failure.

What do you call an elephant who lies across
the middle of a tennis court?
Annette!

30,40

What do you call an
elephant creeping
through the jungle
in the middle of
the night?
Russell!

What do you call an elephant with a seagull on its head?
Cliff!

What do you call an elephant with a rabbit up its sweater?
Warren!

What do you call the rabbit up the elephant's sweater?
Terrified!

What do you call someone with an elephant on their head?
Squashed.

How do elephants speak to each other?
By 'elephone.

What did the zoo keeper say when he saw
three elephants in sunglasses coming over
a hill?
Nothing, he didn't recognize them.

When do elephants have eight feet?
When there are two of them.

How can you tell when there's an elephant under the bed?
When you're nearly touching the ceiling.

What do you give an
elephant with big feet?
Plenty of room.

What do you say when an elephant sits on your sofa?
It's time to get a new sofa!

Why did the elephant walk on two legs?
To give the ants a chance.

Why do elephants have trunks?
Because they have no pockets to put things in.

A man was sprinkling white powder on his lawn.

"Why are you doing that?" asked his neighbour.

"It's to keep the elephants off the grass," replied the first man.

"But we don't get any elephants around here!"

"I know – good stuff, isn't it?"

Which animals were the last to leave the ark?
The elephants, because they had to pack their trunks.

What would happen if an elephant sat in front of you at the movies?
You would miss most of the film.

What steps would you take if you were being chased by an elephant?
Big ones.

What do you find
in an elephant's
graveyard?
Elephantoms.

Why do elephants
have wrinkly ankles?
*Because their shoes are
too tight.*

Which is stronger, an
elephant or a snail?
*A snail, because it
carries its house. An
elephant only carries
its trunk.*

What do you do with
old cannon balls?
*Give them to elephants
to use as marbles.*

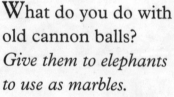

What do elephants
do in the evenings?
Watch elevision.

Who lost a herd of
elephants?
Big Bo Peep.

What is an elephant's
favourite film?
Elephantasia.

What do elephants
say as a compliment?
You look elephantastic!

What did the elephant
say to the famous
detective?
*It's ele-mentary, my
dear Sherlock.*

What is a baby
elephant after he is
five weeks old?
Six weeks old.

What did the elephant say when the man
grabbed him by the tail?
This is the end of me.

Why did the elephant jump in the lake when it began to rain?
To stop getting wet.

What should you do if an elephant breaks down your front door?
Escape through the back door.

How do you raise a baby elephant that has been abandoned by its parents?
With a fork-lift truck.

How do you hire an elephant?
Stand it on four bricks.

"Dad! Mum is fighting with an enormous
elephant in the front garden!"

"Don't worry, dear, I'm sure the elephant
can look after itself."

"I say, I say, I say, my elephant's
got no trunk."
"How does he smell?"
"Terrible!"

How are elephants and
hippopotamuses alike?
Neither can play basketball.

How do you keep an angry elephant from charging?
Take away his credit cards.

What did the baby elephant get when the daddy elephant sneezed?
Out of the way!

Why do elephants have short tails?
They can't remember long stories.

How do you keep an
elephant in suspense?
I'll tell you tomorrow.

Why is an elephant braver than a hen?
Because the elephant isn't chicken.